Debt-Free

Break Free from Debt- the Ultimate Life Hacks to Live without Debt! (Get Out of Debt, Budgeting Money, Save Money, Credit Card Debt, Wealth Management, Credit Control, Money Tips)

By:

James Stevens

Published by Shepal Publishing,

All Rights Reserved

Copyright 2016, New York

Table of Contents

Introduction

Are you in debt? Are you finding it hard to pay off what you owe and move on with your life? Debts will stagnate you and leave you with no way of moving forward in life. Borrowing money is very easy, as well as using your credit card to make payments but when debts accumulate, you realize that it is very hard to pay them off. Getting into debt these days is very easy. There are so many things on offer, as well as services and sellers who are willing to give them on credit to willing buyers. This is what lures many people into debt because they want what is on offer without taking a second to think about how they will pay for things afterwards.

When debts become overwhelming, they can bring a lot of problems not just to you but also to the people in your life. You might end up losing all the material things you have to creditors, as well as your reputation and dignity.

You do not have to wait for that to happen though because paying off your debts is actually quite easy. This eBook provides you with a step by step guide into payment of most types of debts, including credit card debts. Budget for your money, clear off your debts, start saving and manage your wealth and you will have a great future that is financially guaranteed.

Chapter 1:
Life in Debt

Apparently, it is very easy for one to get into debt. Many people seem to slide into debt without realizing it. When debt piles up it seems like an insurmountable mountain that towers over you and leaves you in total confusion. It is incredibly simple to get into debt, in fact, it happens without any thought or real effort. As a human being, it is simple to desire something amazing that you cannot pay for at a given time and because the desire overwhelms you, you opt to borrow in order to have the best of the things that you admire. This happens without you having a true picture of the overall effect on your finances.

Today, people are driven by consumption and manufacturers are not disappointing in their production. It has become very easy to get anything that one desires, irrespective of its price. Sellers are always willing to give consumers what they need for them to pay at a later date and this is what has messed up the lives of a lot of people.

What happens in the end is that all the bills accumulate and a time comes for you to pay them, plus their interest. This is the time the reality shines on your face and you realize that getting out of that debt is not as easy as you imagined it will be. The unfortunate thing is that it will be too late because your debtors will be on your case every day, every hour, every minute. This is the time that you realize that paying off a debt can be a real challenge.

Causes of debt

Other than the desire to own what you cannot easily afford, there are so many other reasons why people find themselves in debt and these are:

i) Income reduction- If your income is reduced and you still have the same expenses, chances are high that you will get into debts in order to cater for your needs. A lot of people are unable to bring down their expenses when their income reduces. They have to find a way to ensure that they are able to cater for everything they need with the amount of income they are getting. Instead, they let debts fill in the gaps. It is important to realize that the sooner you balance your income and expenses, the better it will be for you even if the income reduction is a temporary thing. Always live within your means and you will not have to borrow to cater for your needs and desires.

ii) Poor money management- Everything you do in life needs a proper plan and this includes money. Without a good plan, you will not have any control on how you are spending your money and in the end, one realizes that they do not have any money for the most important needs after they have spent it on other less important things. This is what drives people into debt, because the most important needs have to be met anyway. You should always work with a budget to avoid this.

iii) Gambling- A lot of people are into financial debts because of gambling. Gambling loans are easily available and gambling can be addictive, which is the reason why many people get into debt.

The Effects of Debts

Debts are like illnesses that never go away. They will persevere for a very long time until you decide to take action. Debts will bring along suffering and so much pain to the people who are unable to get out of them. The problem is that no one is immune against debts; this is something that can happen to anyone, any time. So many people have been diagnosed with both physical and mental illnesses because of debts, therefore it is a real issue.

People who were once good have resorted to stealing and conning people just so they can pay off their debts. Others have become liars just so they can hide from their debts. Debts are not easy to deal with and they can drive anyone insane. The results are shame, embarrassment, and depression, anger and even anxiety. Most of these issues are experienced due to massive accumulation of debts. Other effects that come as a result of debts include:

a) Bankruptcy- So many people resort to bankruptcy in order to seek the protection of the law to be able to get off their debts once and for good. Filing for bankruptcy is not an easy decision and has far reaching consequences but it may be a viable option when one has no way out of debt.

b) Foreclosure- This will happen if you are not able to pay off your mortgage loan. This means that you end up losing the home you had already bought and maybe the amount of money you had already paid to your mortgage lender.

c) Eviction- Renters who are in debts and unable to pay off their rents on time may face eviction. If this happens, you will be left with no place to live.

d) Salary garnishment- If your creditors sue you, they might have your salary or wages garnished and this means that you will be working for no pay in order to get out of debt. Your salary will automatically be sent to those whom you owe to pay off your debt in full.

e) Emotional effects- The emotions of a person in debts do not remain the same. Even the happiest person becomes sad because of the pressure of clearing debts and also the embarrassment debts bring. Your creditors will contact you all the time reminding you to do your part to pay off the debts. In some cases, you may even have to deal with threats.

f) Suicide attempts- A lot of people commit suicide when they realize that there is no way they will ever be able to pay off their debts. So much pressure from your creditors can drive someone to their grave. Some people feel that dying is the only way they will deal with all their problems once and for good without realizing how many problems they cause their families.

Chapter 2:
Step by Step guide to Becoming Debt Free

Debts will always feel heavy even if it is just a small amount of money. The problem is that people accumulate so many debts before they even start thinking of how much money they owe others. With so many debts, you will always feel like you are carrying a very heavy load around your neck. A good way to start is to come face to face with the reality; you need to confront your debts head on so that you will know just how much money you owe others. This way, coming up with a strategy to pay back your debts will be easy.

Managing your debts can be a challenge, whether your debt is ten dollars or ten thousand dollars. Do you want to get under your debts? Here is a step by step guide that can help you stay debt free:

1. Assess your problems: You have to face your debts if you want to get out of them and the first thing is to assess just how much debt you are into. You cannot afford to give up on debts because your creditors will not forget the fact that you owe them money. Coming to terms with just how much money you owe will make it easy to plan on how you can pay back the money. What you do is to list down all the debts you have accumulated and get the total amount. Make sure that you leave nothing out.

2. Give the high interest debts the first priority- With the list of all the debts, you need to start looking closer to see how many of the costly debts you have and if there

are the less costly debts. If the debts that accumulate interest stay longer without being cleared, you might end up paying so much more, that is why they should be prioritized, then you can pay off the less expensive debts afterwards.

3. Come up with a plan to pay off the debts- Do this in consideration with the amount of income you are receiving. You should also state clearly how much money you are receiving as income so that you will work against your debts to see the best way forward in clearing the debts. You can for instance start by paying off all the prioritized debts first, as you make minimal payments for the other debts, then go down the list until you are free of all the debts. This is the only way you will gain total control over your debts. If all your debts require the same amount of attention, start with the smallest debt going up. This way, you will be happy with how fast you are able to pay off your debts and this will motivate you to go on until all the debts are cleared.

4. Seek financial advice- Good news is that you do not have to go through the stress of getting off your debts alone; financial advisors always offer help to those people in need of help especially if their debts are mainly from loans. Loans are very complicated to deal with especially if you want to pay them off as fast as possible, that is why the help of a financial advisor will be important. One of the things that a financial advisor will help you with is in consolidating your debts into one large debt that will be easier to manage, with a lower interest charge.

With the help of a financial advisor, you can negotiate for a lower interest charge or a more manageable repayment pattern so as to have an easier time paying back the loans. This way, you will pay your debts back without worrying that they will be getting bigger every day that passes.

5. Create a strict budget to have more money for debt payment- One of the things that people should learn is how to live within their means. When you are in debt, you should set your mind that you only have a small amount of money to live on and this should be enough for most of your important needs. With a budget, you should be able to see just how much money you are spending on food, on rent and other necessary bills. See how you can reduce some of the money from those categories in order to increase the amount of money you are allocating to debts. If you do not have enough money coming in, you have only two choices; to either make more money or to reduce your expenses accordingly.

6. Cut costs wherever possible- What you should be aiming at right now is to devote as much money as possible to debt repayment therefore you have to do what you can so as to have more money going to your creditors. There is always a way you can cut down the cost of certain items and needs that you pay for every month. You can for instance cut down on the cost of foods that you cook every day. If for buy ready meals, you can reduce the cost considerably by buying ingredients cheaply and making your meals at home.

Consider cutting down on the cost of entertainment too. In as much as this is important in your life, you can forego a few things for a while in order to get out of debt. Channel all that money to repayment of debts and the debt balances will go down every month. Before you know it, you will be able to spend on all the things you love again.

7. Whenever you come into some unexpected money, pay a little more to your debts instead of blowing it away like many people do. When you have extra, many people think of things they can buy or pay for in order to spoil themselves a little. You should be thinking of how much difference it will make in the end if you channeled that extra money to payment of your debts. This is how you will get off your debts faster.

8. Save every penny that you do not spend- Sometimes people get into debts because they have not saved some money for emergency needs. Once you have budgeted for your expenses and you realize that there is a little more that is left, save it for the emerging needs, incidents and other expenditure and you will never go back into debts.

9. After paying all your debts, you have to purpose to live debt free. This is very easy if you make up your mind not to buy things that you cannot afford. One of the rules many people live by is if they cannot pay anything by cash, they do not need it. That is why they are able to stay free of debts.

You do not have to live like a miser in order to stay out of debts though; you just have to ensure that you are saving some money for anything extra that you will need, for instance a vacation or an expensive phone. If you keep paying your debts on time and you keep up with the saving, you will never get into any debts. Above all, live within your means. There is no need to buy something that other people have if you cannot afford it.

Chapter 3:
Budgeting

One of the things that will help you manage your finances well to stay out of debt is budgeting. With a budget, you can pay off your debts, save up for the future and enjoy a better life because your money will be taking care of all your needs however little it is. The kind of budget you should create is one that reflects your income; some people will budget for less and others will budget for more. With a properly written budget, you should be able to make the best financial decisions that will free you from debts and give you lasting happiness.

Analyzing your income and expenses

The first thing you need to do is to come to terms about how much money you are receiving as income every month. This will be the basis for your budget.

You need to track down just how much you spend in a month. Gather your past bills, your past bank and credit card statements, the receipts you have used in the past and anything else that will help you get an estimate of just how much money you spend in a month. Make a list of your expenses in the order of priority and put an estimate amount on each end so as to know how much you need for a particular need.

A personal budgeting software

Today, budgeting for personal finances is becoming much easier thanks to the help of budgeting software. This is a new trend in finance that is slowly becoming popular because people need help to get out of debt faster. The software comes with budget making tools that are built-in, which can help you personalize your budget. Some also come with analytics that can help you understand your spending habits better, so that you can make better decisions for a better future. Some of these software are:

- Quicken
- Mint
- Microsoft Money
- BudgetPulse
- AceMoney
- BudgetPulse

A spreadsheet

If you do not want to use a budgeting software, you can always create your own budget on a spreadsheet. What is important is that you are able to see clearly what your income amount is and what your expenses amount to in maybe a year. With clear information, you can always tell the areas where you are spending more than you should, so that you can cut down on the expenditure to have more savings. This is how you create a simple yearly budget in a spreadsheet:

✓ Start by labelling the cells from top with the 12 months of the year

✓ Create expenses in the columns, grouping them together in order to have a clearer budget and to avoid confusion.

✓ List down all your expenses on the columns, which are the bills you have to pay, groceries, entertainment, shopping and anything else that you spend money on every month. You should consider all your expenses in at least a year so as to have a clear view of all your expenses.

Note the following:

There are two types of expenses:

a. Fixed expenses: these are the regular monthly expenses that you have to cater for and they include all the bills you pay for every month, the shopping you do, the household products you require every month, the insurance, loans, food among others.

b. Discretionary Expenses: these are the expenses that are usually not fixed and they may be optional. These are for instance savings, entertainment, vacations and other luxuries that you only pay for when you have more money to spend.

When analyzing your expenses versus revenue, you have to make sure that your revenue is more than your expenses, otherwise you are living beyond your means. You should be able to cater for all your expenses with the money you receive as income and maybe have some money left in the end.

Budget creation

With all the information gathered above, you should be able to create a preliminary budget. Add some money, maybe 5% more to each category to cater for the changes in prices of items and increase in the cost of some services so that you will not have to run out of money before you meet all your needs.

If you have some money left every month after you have met all your needs in the budget, you need to budget for it as well. You can for instance choose to save some of the money in an emergency savings fund, you can choose to save all of it in your savings account, you can chose to use some or all of the money in paying back your debts or you can budget to use some of the money to pay for a vacation.

Everything you have on your budget should be very clear and actionable so as to make it easy for you to stick to the budget requirements to the end.

Becoming a budgeting expert

Creating a budget is very easy but you have to ensure that you stick to it. This is what makes you a budgeting pro. The most important thing here is to stick to the budget all the way and to avoid overspending. People love buying and spending money, which is why many people end up breaking the simple rule of not overspending. Most of the time you realize that when you overspend, the money does not go towards anything good, and this is highly regrettable especially if you end up getting into debts for this.

Always work hard to reduce your expenses without denying yourself some of the most important needs. You can for instance skip a vacation one year in order to save some money for an important project. You can also go for less expensive items to cut down the cost so as to afford much of what you need.

Treat yourself from time to time, but not all the time. You should have a good reason to do this and ensure that it is not affecting your budget in any way. This way, you will be happy to stick to the rules.

Chapter 4:
Saving Money

Everyone is driven by instant pleasure these days, explaining why many people are getting into debt without necessarily showing how they are spending the money that they borrow. This is the reason why it is very important to learn how to save money any way you can, however little it is because it can help you acquire that item you really need without getting into debts for it.

Saving is not very easy especially for low income earners. There are people who believe that saving is only possible for people who earn so much money in a month, which is not the case. Anyone can save; you just need to monitor how you are spending your money and cut down on your expenditure and you will have something left every month for saving. Saving can be a daily thing if you are devoted to it and it can make a huge difference in the way that you will live your life thereafter. Here is how:

1) Have a weekly money date- You have to set some time aside every week to evaluate your budget, to review your accounts and also to see how you are progressing with the financial goals that you have already set. This is very important because you will be able to see if you are on the right track or not as far as your budget is concerned. In case of a problem, it is easy to fix it earlier when this is done weekly and this will prevent long-term financial issues that could get you into so many financial problems. Spending more time with your money will make it easy for you to know what you need to change so as to have enough to save for a rainy season.

2) Make a weekly plan for your meals- You only need a few hours in a week to buy everything that you will require for your meals for the entire week and this will save you a lot of money. This will cancel the likelihood of dining out for instance, which is the main reason people spend so much money in a month. Buying groceries in bulk will also save you a lot of money and once this is done, you will not have to keep spending money on a daily basis.

3) Make your coffee at home- Going to coffee shops for the best coffee is something that a lot of people love but imagine just how much money you spend on that daily. It will be more economical to make coffee at home and save money afterwards. If you love the organic coffee they serve in coffee shops, you can treat yourself to that once in a while then make your own coffee at home the rest of the days.

4) Make more money- If you feel that you do not have enough money to save, you should make more money. Work more as this is the only way you will make enough for all your expenses. Also, working more leaves you with less time to spend and this is a great way to save your money. If you can, get busy and you will not have to worry about how much money you are spending in a day.

5) Learn some DIY skills- There is so much that you can do for yourself yet you spend so much money on it. Everyone is creative in their own sense. You can save so much money on gifts that you can creatively make at home. You can also fix your own locks or appliances

instead of paying someone else to do it. There is a lot of information online today that can help you do so much on your own without necessarily calling and paying for help. This will save you so much money.

The benefits of saving

Saving is good for your health and also for your finances. If you find yourself spending all your money before the end of the month, maybe it is time to consider saving. You need just a little money every month and so many benefits will come your way:

- Saving will reduce a lot of your stress: not having enough money for all your needs can bring enough stress in your life. Sometimes it is hard to deal with the fact that what you are getting is not even enough for the things that you need in life. It leads to depression, anxiety, insomnia and sometimes heart related issues. Saving will help reduce this kind of stress because you know that if anything comes after you have already spent money on your paycheck, you will be able to handle it.

- Saving gives you a great relief. It makes you feel saner, the same way you feel when you realize that you have total control of things in your life. With some saved money, you worry less because you will not be moved by any emergency that will come your way since you can handle them and this makes you feel better.

- Saving money makes you happier- without money, your happiness fades away but when you realize that you have some money somewhere, you will always feel happy even if you are not spending it at that time. This way, you can make better decisions in life and you can work more and better for more.

- Saving can help you stay healthy-In order to save, you choose to eat at home and not out and this is one way through which you can enjoy healthier meals for a healthy life thereafter. You are also able to cut down on things that do not contribute much to your health and this boosts your health in the end. You start walking for instance in order to save on cab fare and this boosts your health too.

- You are prepared for emergencies- Only a few people are able to deal with emerging needs and this means that only a few people save. When you save money, you are able to deal with any emerging stuff without getting into debts. This is great and it gives you peace of mind knowing that there is nothing that will be too much for you to handle.

Chapter 5:
Credit Card Debt

Credit cards are great but only if they are used wisely. This is not easy though because a lot of people find it hard to stop buying and desiring more yet they do not have the ability to pay for it. In the end, they are met with huge credit card bills to settle. So many people in the country today are dealing with very high credit card debts and they have no way of paying them back. There are so many reasons why you would have accumulated so much debts and interest charges but what is important now is to get rid of these debts once and for good. This will be a major step to take in order to get out of debt in life and enjoy financial freedom in the end. But how can this be achieved?

There are so many strategies that can help you get rid of your credit card debts if you are keen on it. You need to come up with a good pan and stick to it and then you will see how easy this can be, irrespective of how much money you we your credit card company. Here are some of these strategies:

Deal with one card at a time

Many people have more than one credit card and the most likely thing is that you have debts on all your cards. If this is so, it will not be easy to pay off all the debts in all the cards at the same time; you have to start with one card, then the other until all the debts are cleared. Start with the card with the lowest debt then channel as much money as you can towards repayment of the debts on that card. Once this is done, you will see how easy it is to get out of credit card debts and this should keep you going until all the debts are cleared off. Another strategy you can use here is to pay off debts on a card that has high interest charges. This way, you will not be left paying so much more in the end.

Negotiate for lower interest charges

A lot of credit card companies are always willing to give their creditors a lower interest charge if they are willing to clear off the debts in the shortest time possible. If this is possible, you will be left paying less than you would have paid in the first place. This will make paying off the debts much easier. This works best if you have been their customer for a while and if your credit score is good though.

Use cheaper loans

Credit cards are very expensive to maintain. The interests charged by credit companies are very high, therefore the more you stay in debt, the more you will end up paying in the end. You can opt for a cheaper loan with a much lower interest charge to clear off your debts, then you are left with a smaller loan to pay off. There are so many secure sites online which offer reliable loans at fixed interest charges, which are much easier to deal with than credit card debts.

Aim to make a minimum of two payments every month

Credit card interests are charged according to the amount of money that you owe the credit card company. If you have a large balance, you will be paying more than the person with a smaller balance, which is why it is important to reduce your balance as much as you can. You are to work harder and make a minimum of two payment every month in order to reduce your balances considerably every month. This is also the fastest way to get off credit card debts.

Credit card debt consolidation

Credit card debt consolidation is something that a lot of financial advisors will advise you to go for if you have a large amount of debt to clear off. This entails adding up all the debts that you have into one single and new debt, of a much lower interest rate, which is easier to pay off than the previous multiple debts. Not all people succeed in debt consolidation though, therefore you have to be sure that it will work for you before you take this option.

Debt consolidation is a much better plan that will allow you to gain control over your finances, therefore it is a good option to consider if you really want to get out of debt faster and easier. The first step to take is to consider if it will work for you. The main factor to consider here is the cash that you have at hand. Here are some of the things that will determine if consolidating your debt will work for you or not:

> Are you serious about getting out of debt? Debt consolidation should only be used if you are planning to

get out of debt as fast as possible. If not, there is no need to consolidate your debts as they will be more overwhelming and difficult to pay off in the end.

➤ Are your debts manageable? This depends on your income and expense amount. If you are left with some money every month after catering for all your expenses, you will be able to pay out of debt but if your income is not even enough to cater for your needs, paying off such debts will be little challenging. You have to work to boost your income first before consolidating your debts.

Chapter 6:
Wealth Management

Every person has his own dreams and desires in life. There are people who yearn for a big house for instance, others want to own a luxurious car and others only want to have a great life that is the envy of a lot of people. This explains why people work really hard every day, because they want to achieve their dreams someday. However, the truth of the matter is that everything that you desire is not really easy to achieve even with so much hard work. You have to pay attention to the most important thing, which is personal wealth management.

What does this mean? Personal wealth management entails taking the right paces at the right time in order to achieve financial solidity. This is what guarantees a safe and happy future as far as your finances are concerned. With a stable future, it can be very easy for one to get exactly what they have been dreaming of, that is why you need to start working towards personal wealth management. Here are some important tips that should get you started:

1. Have a clear plan for your income and expenditure- One of the things that people do not pay attention to is just how much money they receive every month. Is it what you deserve to be paid or do you need to work harder for more? Being underpaid can affect your finances so much thereafter, therefore you have to ensure that you are receiving the right income. When planning for your income, you should be aware of all the income that you receive from different sources every month. This way, you will not overlook any small amount of money that can be very significant in your plan. With the income in perspective, write down all

your expenses and determine where you will cut it out from your income. The rest of the money can be saved.

2. Pay close attention to your savings- There are so many ways through which people save, for instance through investing in the real estate market, purchase of jewelry and other important items to buy. However, you need to pay attention to your cash reserves too because they are as important as anything else. This is the money that will help you in case of emergencies. The best way to ensure that you are saving some money every month is to automate it. This is easy to do these days. You can always ensure that a certain percentage of your income goes to a separate savings account every month even before you get the money, because after that, it can be hard to keep up with the saving. Choose an account that earns you interest so as to grow your savings with time.

3. Set realistic financial goals- You do not have to build so much wealth in a short period of time, even when you are earning so much money. You need to take a step at a time into personal wealth management. If for instance you want to buy a home. You need to take time to save all the money that you will need for a good home. Do not rush things because this is what leads one into unnecessary debts that become difficult to pay off in the end. Set goals in progression; do not mix up the things that you want to do in life. You need to list everything down, then plan on achieving them one after the other as per their importance.

4. Borrow money only when you are sure about paying it back- Loans are really not bad; they are only bad if you are unable to pay them off. There are people who have

done so much in life through loans and they are able to pay their loans on time. If you are sure that you will keep up with the repayments, you can always go for a loan in order to finance something major that you need in life. There is a lot that one can do with a loan, but only if you have the ability to pay back the borrowed money. Good thing about borrowing and paying back on time is that you build your credit history, which will help you in case you will need an important loan thereafter in life. Loan lenders have more faith in people who have a good credit history, which is why this is important.

5. You need a good retirement plan- Many people are so engrossed in the present that they barely think of what will happen when they are no longer able to work. You need to start planning for your retirement today so that you will have a good reserve that you can count on for those days that you will not be receiving any income. You need a long term financial plan that includes days after retirement so that you will not have to depend on other people for financial support after your retirement. Good thing is that many people have good plans for retirement in their workplaces. If you are not contributing to any at the moment, you need to start one as soon as possible.

Wealth management may seem difficult but it is not; you just need to make a few changes in the way that you manage your finances and you will have a stable future to look forward to. The most important thing is to get started right now. Postponing this may mean that you may never get started at all. Do not aim to start at a high note, because it is easy to give up along the way; start slow and start saving more as the time goes by and your future will be financially guaranteed.

Conclusion

Human beings have been created in such a manner that they always want instant satisfaction, therefore they rarely think about the future. Anything that they do is for the immediate fulfilment which explains why so many people get into debts, because they want to get their hands on that which they desire at that moment. The problem with this is that you end up with so many debts to pay off in the future, which is not an easy to deal with especially if the future catches up with you.

When you finally realize that you have accumulated so many debts and you do not have a way to pay them back, stress start creeping in and you lose motivation to work and even to plan on how you will pay out of debt.

It is very easy to get into debt. Sometimes people borrow money when they are sure that they will be able to pay it back soon but something happens along the way and they are unable to meet the end of their bargain. Other people borrow when they are sure they will never be able to pay back the money but they keep hoping that a solution will come up as the days go by.

What is important is coming to terms with the debts you have accumulated and purposing to pay out of debt in full. This is the only way you will enjoy peace of mind in life. You will also be able to start working towards financial freedom and wealth management.

www.ingramcontent.com/pod-product-compliance
Lightning Source LLC
Chambersburg PA
CBHW071834200526
45169CB00018B/1478